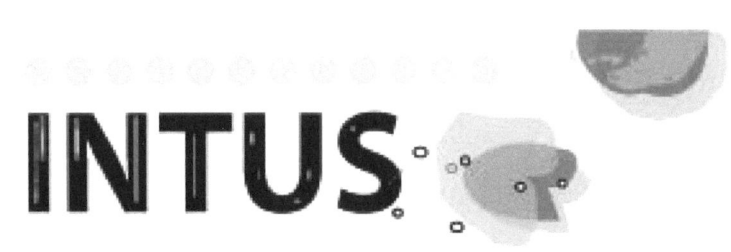

INTUS.

SPIRITUS INTUS ALIT IS
The Spirit nourishes within

*A collection of poetry
& artistic works
made on a journey
to creative freedom*

By
Ava Leigh Stewart

If I have seen further, it is by
standing on the shoulders of
giants.

— *Sir Issac Newton*

TABLE OF CONTENTS

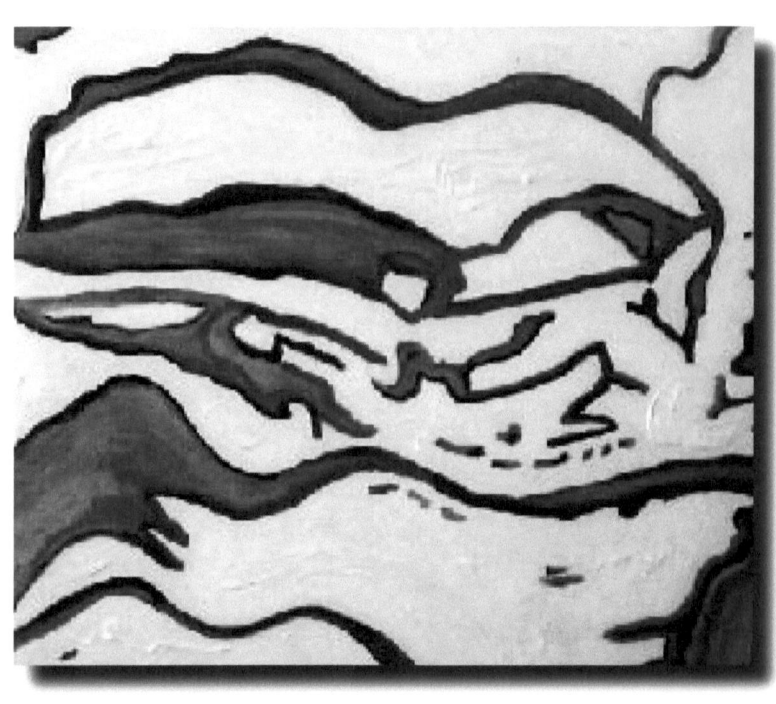

FADO

I took the risk
in the hard unforgiving sun
burned and blistered
waiting for the moment of truth
with wonder and imagination
before surrendering hope

Back again with new ferver
I walked into the door
 not a modern bore
my mind thrives in history
a vast dreaming imagination
an amalgam, hard to sell
new stories to tell

My destiny stands with determination
times that are down trodden
lead us only upward
headed back to the middle
to work for the highest riddle
climb Kilamanjaro before the glacier melts
go to new depths with knowledge
read between the lines to see
THE LINES...

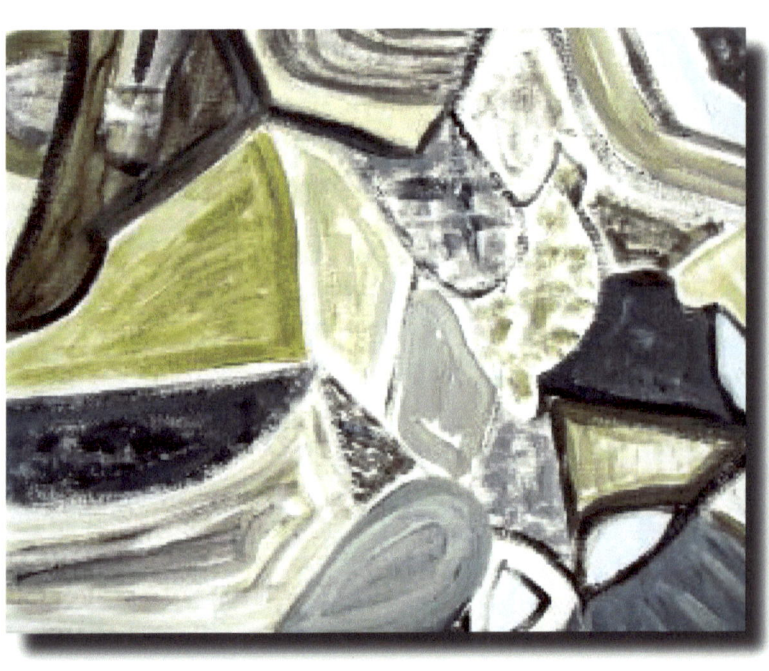

HARPETH NARROWS

I stood near the bank of the river
reflecting in the ruin, the moon's sliver

This land is as old as America
a place time forgot
small reminder of existence
where the White Bluffs glisten in the distance

Always listening silently
never uttering the first syllable
The stories they would rekindle

The rocks started to succumb to the elements
as did the people

Their souls travel in the wind
to all corners of the earth.
They linger on the land
their voices echo.

The people, the times they lived,
the mystery and the mystical place remain.
There are so many ghost stories
dancing in the moonlight.

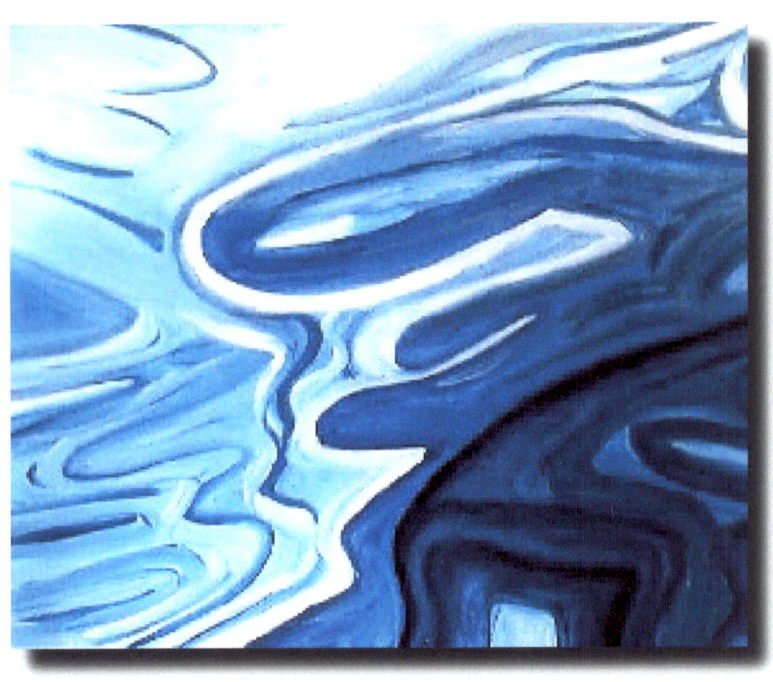

VITA

I'm so tired I can't sleep
I pray my lord my soul to keep
There is a special place in hell
For those that try to sell
The souls of the dying
To the highest bidder

Don't think you know me
You don't know what I want to hear
Own up to your actions
And stop trying to be clear
I will stand here until the end of time
To make sure you don't make a dime

If you have the ability
You have the responsibility
A fight that you didn't make
Is a chance you have to take?
Against the idolatries in society
Down the drain of impurity
Comes rebirth

If I could only say one thing
I wouldn't have the words
In my black hole of Calcutta
I wash water writhed in guilt
With beautiful immorality

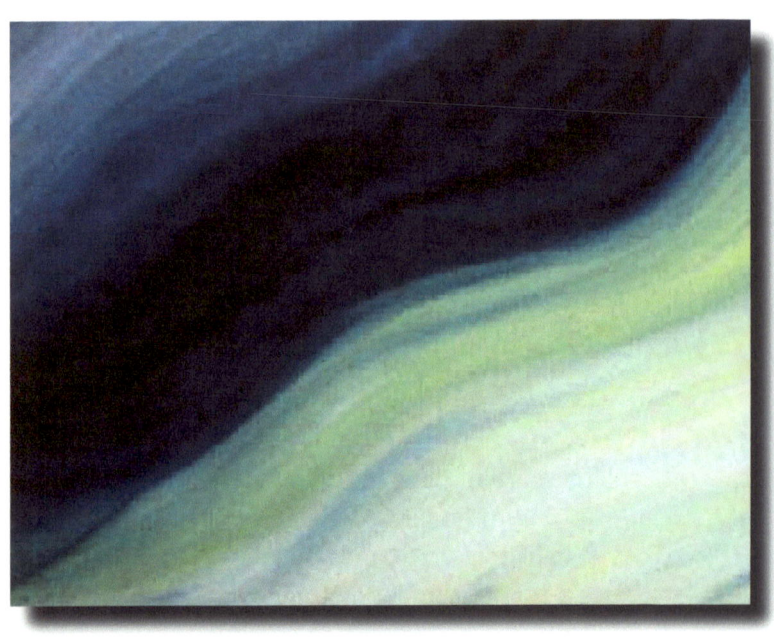

THE MAJESTIC

The wind hit her face as she heard the faint whistle
of the wind rolling on the water
The tide rushed across
As she glared into its depths
As though she was alone, but someone
.....Watched her every move

It had been months since she said goodbye to him
She had a clear picture in her mind..
as she drifted to sleep

It was dawn creeping over the majestic mountains
The height of them
could not match the temptation of the abyss
Something free unleashed
The sea crashed against the rocks
moist drops hit her face and she no longer feared
The sun rose over the majestic mountains

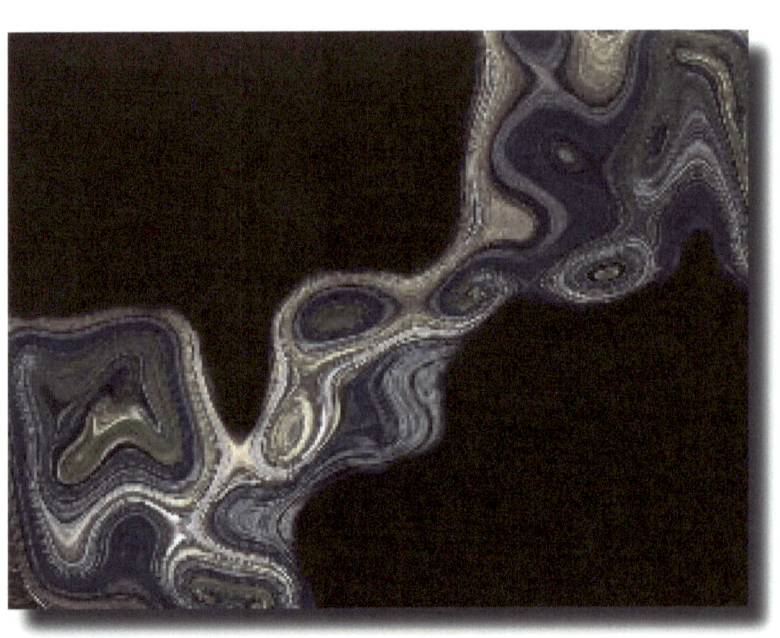

MEDIO

Do you know it is I?
Do you see me in your dreams?

I hope to find my ray
of sun between the seams.

So I can be
The person you see

A counterpart
the truth of heart

Half of your soul.
You are mine.

I wish for you
my life embued

Soul
Heart
Love

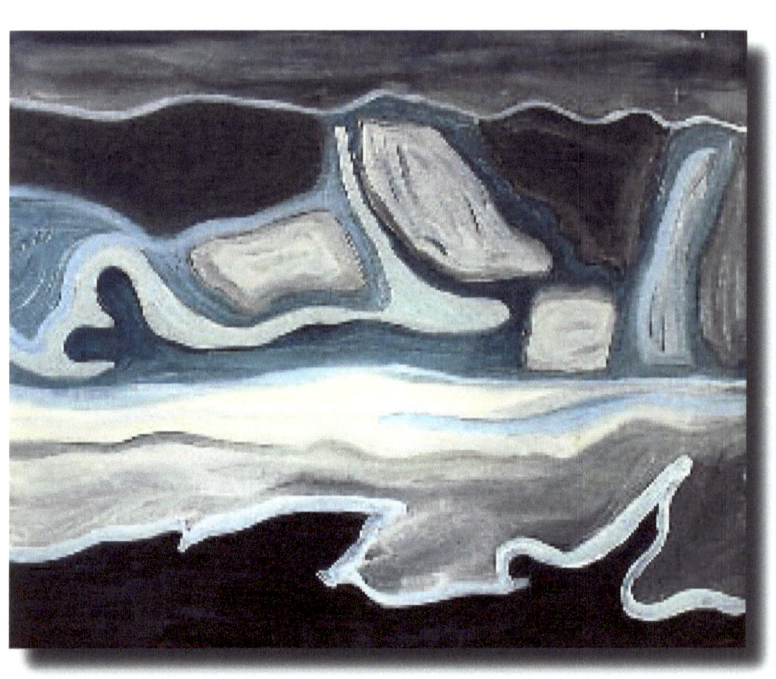

MOMENTS

Was he thinking about me when he looked out
into the distance?

The awkward silence on the mountaintop.
An amorous smile. I left, even though I knew.

I took the slower way down the mountain.
Defying my nature and my destiny.
Does he wait for me?

Does he remember the moment we met?
I am resolute to be grateful for that one moment.
It was I who let go of the attachment.

Love will never be true if it is attached.
I do have remorse. I am angry not to live in the
present. I retrace the steps of that day, agonize
over the moment. Although I think I should not.

 The energy could linger forever - neverending
and appearing again.

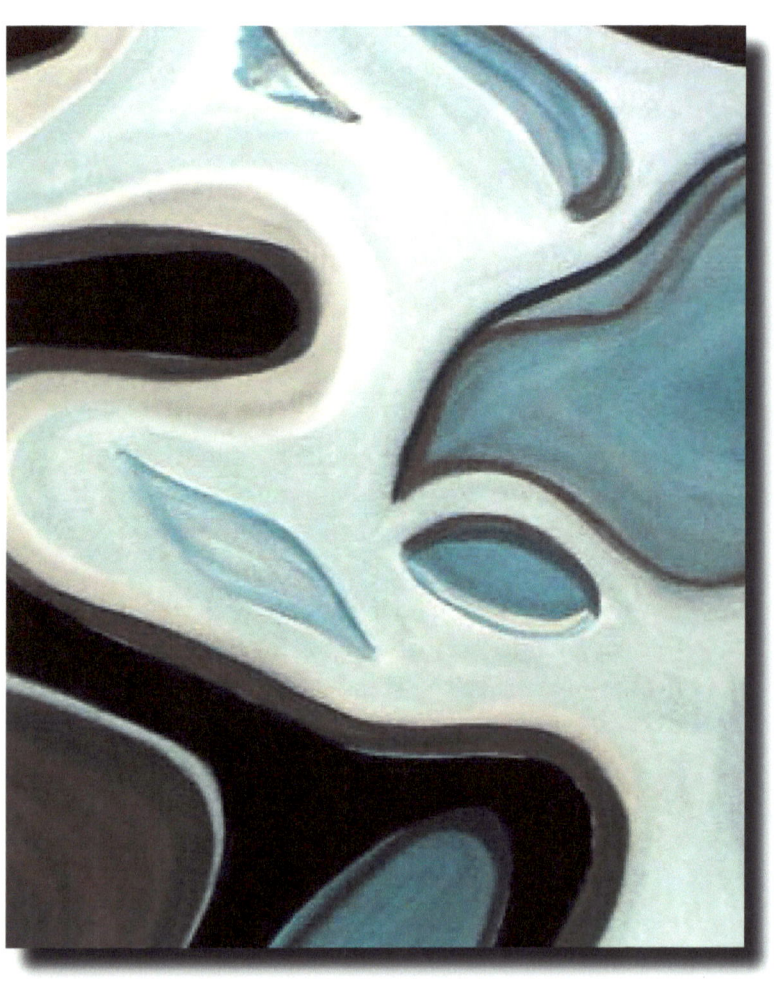

NOTHING

I have thought about you all day
the wine from Italy
the fire in your eyes

I thought of all the ones I lost
the opportunity cost

the one that I cannot let go
all the others I can forgo

Dismissing you for some time
desperate not to pine

did I love you above others?
finding it hard to start again
day and night I see your face.

will my life be changed by unrequited love?
Do you seem fonder as the time passes?

more affection than you deserve
betray me, unwillingly and without reserve

What is there left of me without you?

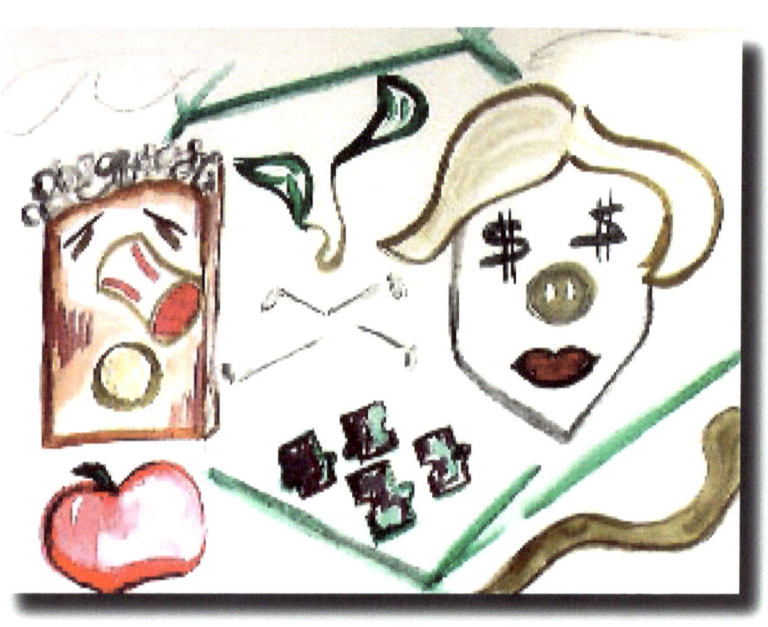

RANT OF A CHILD

House stager? Paid?
The fabric that was for where? Freudian Slip
Birthday card – left   DVD – Left
Note – Unread
Home in Shambles
Bought a Bike without even asking...
Golf, no time, Golf, Golf, and more Golf
Sprinkler Disaster
Trash in Garage
Never   remembers   anything – how convenient?
Ignores his own father in his older age
Lead around by the nose like a prepubescent
schoolboy
What is the story?
Decorative ornamentation?
Is that what children become?
Lies, extortion, fraudulent, suck up, asshole.
Make fun of me with his friends...
how big can you be?
Sex maniac
No common sense
Ask permission for lunch?
Slap a waiter with a knife
Masturbate in front of the whole family...
How can I forgive?

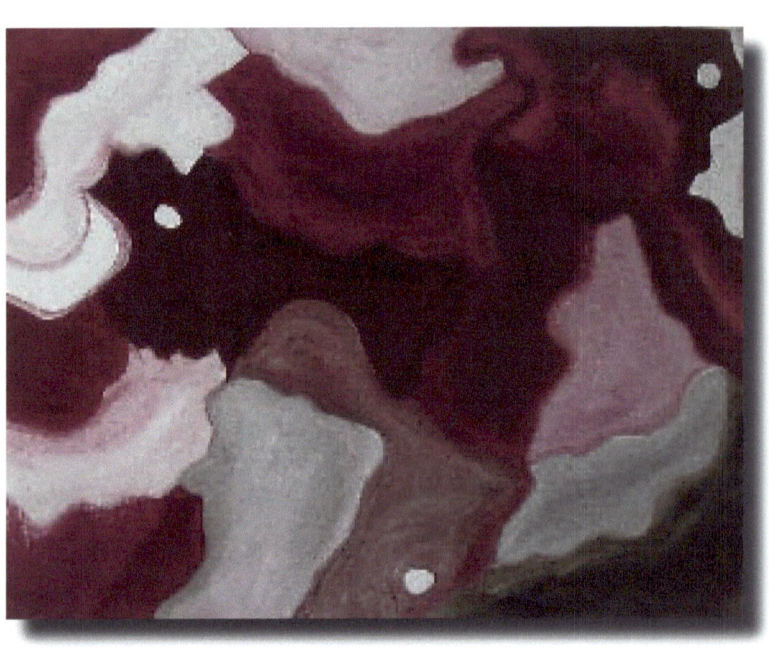

SPRING BOUQUET

Years later as I sat in the midst of the field behind her house, it was like yesterday when I was a child. Suddenly, time was frozen, I crossed from the green grass and picturesque houses into a whole new world only a stream's jump away.

The wind gently blew the cool air and the smell of spring. The sunlight made the days feel so alive, as it reflected off the daffodils that grew feely amongst the grass. The daffodils I waited to pick every visit. I would spend hours in that field, everyday I could, picking the flowers.

Sometimes when I go there it is as if the wind could be her watching over us as she had for so long. I wished I could give her a spring bouquet, but I had gathered nothing, I was motionless. Instead, I sat listening to the birds sing, the leaves rustle, and the wind blow through the grass.

The flowers grew untouched and I took a deep breath. The flowers would remain beautiful for everyone to enjoy and there would not be a Spring Bouquet. She always told me that she was looking forward to seeing me soon, as she waved, when I left.

Today, I believe she said goodbye.

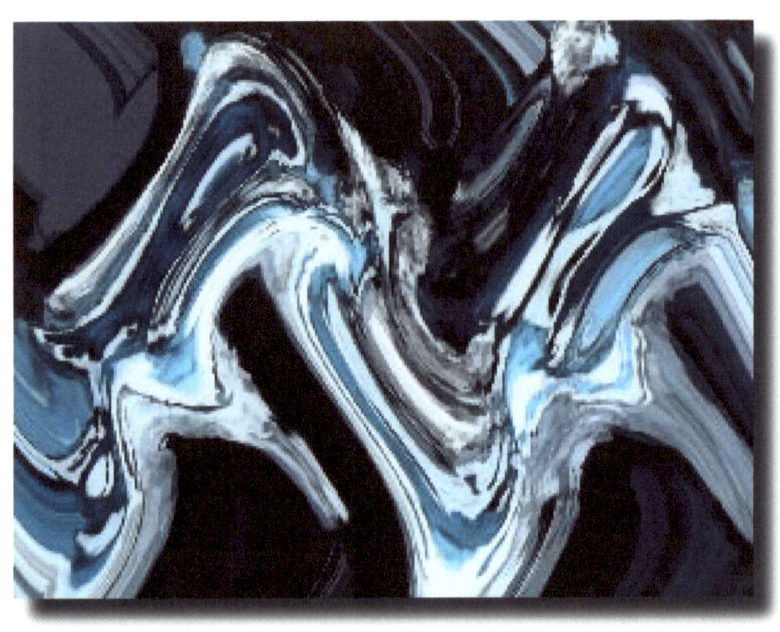

THE NOMAD

He wanders aimlessly toward a new
life with no lack of ambition
Able to see resilience in new beginnings,
a chance to explore worlds
that have never been traveled

Beyond the sails,
land resting abreast the tranquility
of the ocean
which hath no fury
He crawled toward the destination
that would leave security with reason

A place of subtle riches
that would provide happiness
in its simplicity.
Looking back, there is no horizon
like that which you have made.

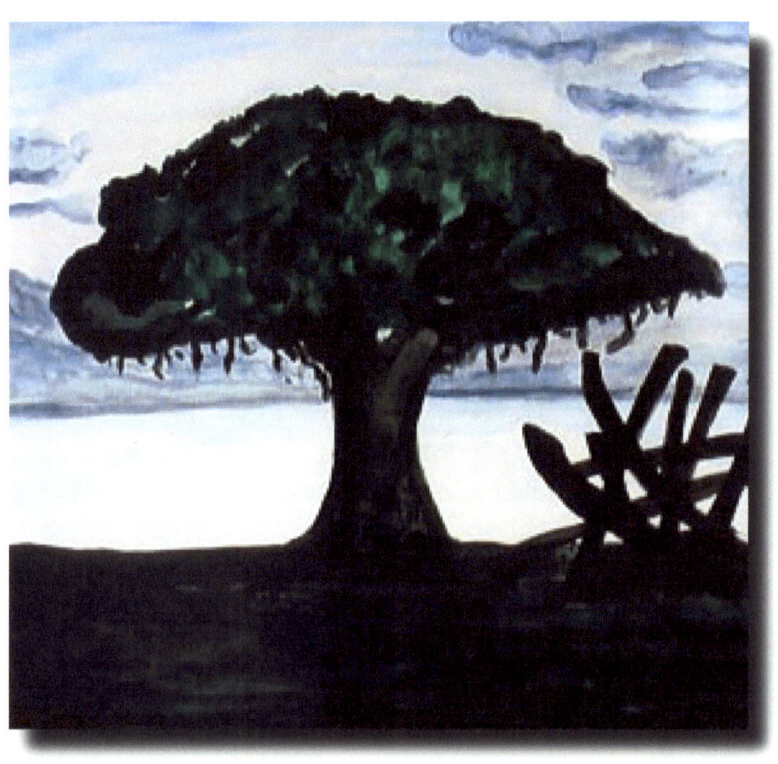

PERSEVERANCE

The freezing cold on their skin
what if it was the antediluvian?
Trapped since the great flood
making their way from the universe

What is the message?
Do our ancestors defend their passage?
Is this the battle of purgatory?
To save humanity from itself

Earth is utopia to everything
Powers at work so aggressive
forget humanity for the sake of greed
On the edge, the end creeps..
Population has doubled six times
Fossil fuels to blame?

Fossils will not last
Life moves past
Work in unity
What if all we know was gone tomorrow?
We have to beat impunity
Every choice is important
Imagine the future for our children
Perseverance

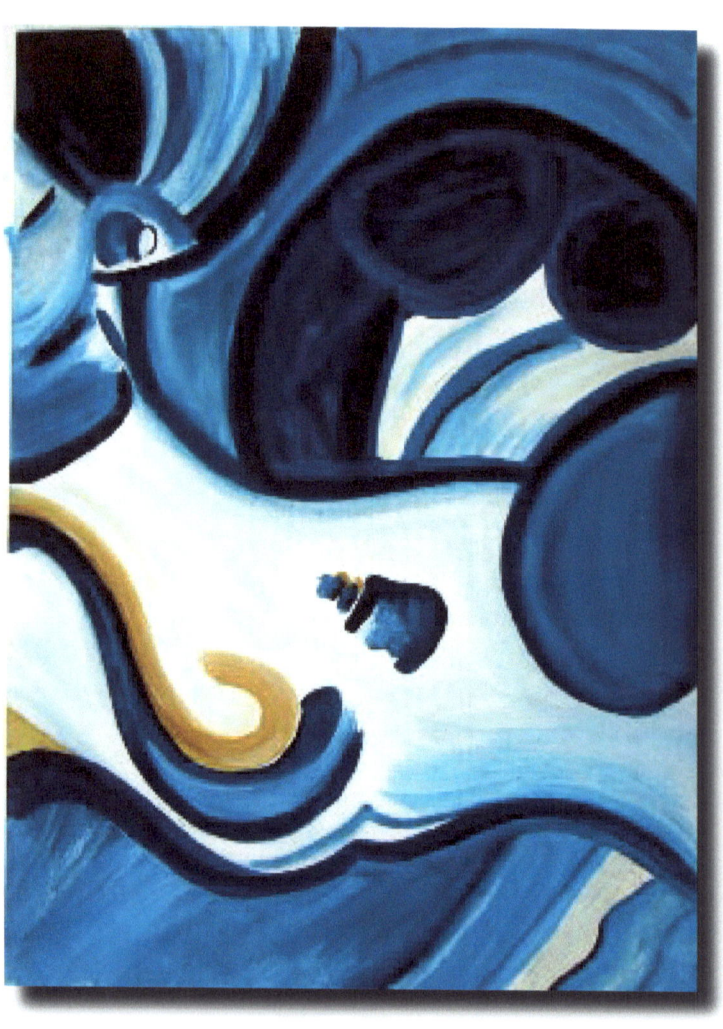

VENICE

Crash of water against the rocks
constant like a never-ending fight.

sharp whistle of wind travels
moist sea spurt becomes heavy rain

No light will lead the ship
the city a black hole of wet darkness.

Air is thick and hot
until a breeze sweeps
into the narrow streets.

a moment later
stagnation returns

in the midst of the ancient buildings
time is untouched by motion

the buildings the same as old
from one street to the next

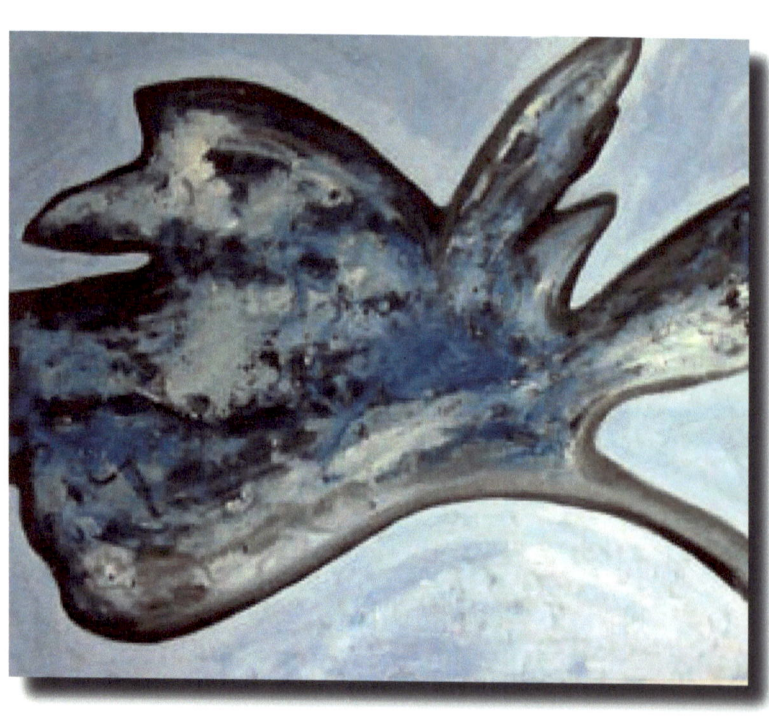

FEAR

I do not fear the road ahead.
there will be obstacles
I will find a way to cross the stream.

Fear keeps the water dammed
Also flowing uncontrollably

I cannot fear the water inside of me.
the exposure, opening free
to a tsunami of pain
the feeling is life changing.

Some things are not explained by logic.
the water of life is uncharted.
I am required to trust.

Falling into the water naked.
I will reach the shore
following the current of life

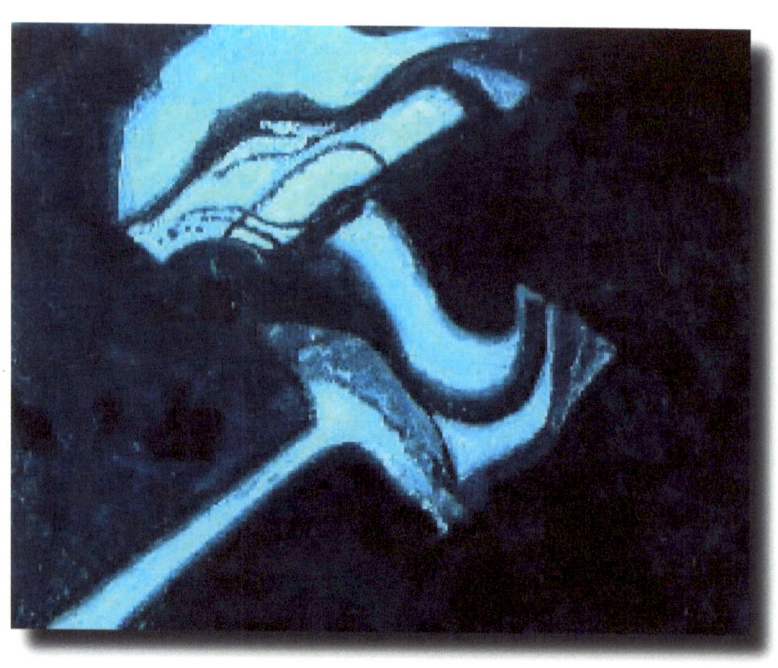

LIVES PAST

Strange forces are at work
Evil & Greed seem to usurp

An energy that numbs the mind
And makes us forgetful

Only glimpses of truth
From those that have no cooth

The chosen elite
Never cut their teeth

Living off the fear of the masses
several milenna passes

Not all time has been this way
we have all been lead astray

Always is motion
Energy is an undulating ocean

The tides wash the shore
And these times will be no more

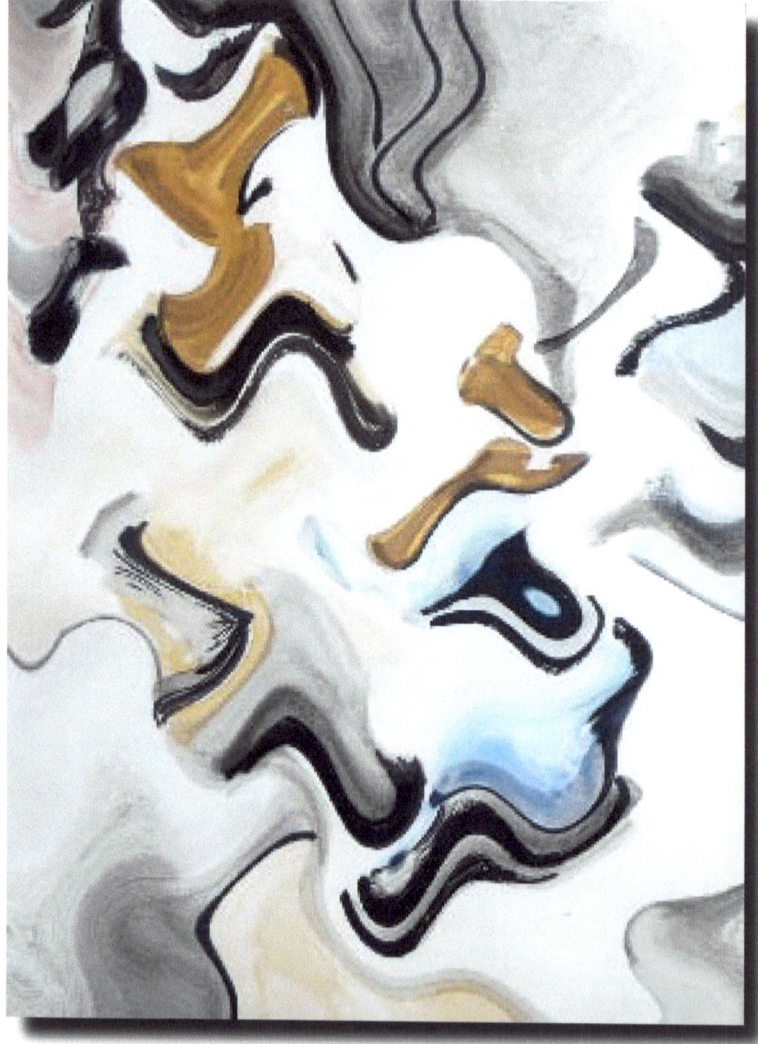

ANOTHER REALM

The moon steals the light from the sun
only for a short time until daylight

never-ending cycle of theft
the realm in which time exists

the flame is fueled
then extinguished

enigma of form
represents nothing

no sound will describe
a blank mirrored vortex

never a future meeting
existence is fleeting

mysterious feeling of amazement

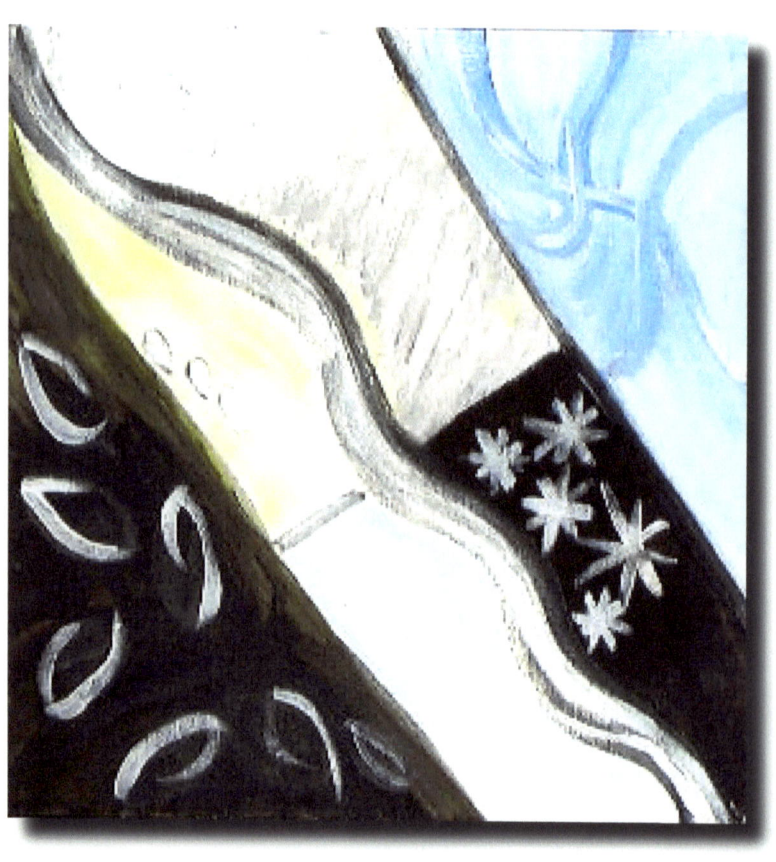

LONDON

Dare to Fail and you might succeed
Something unknown that you need

Bottom feeders attach like crustaceans
Soar above meaningless interations

Never ending from the beginning
Something that you find witting

Sit frozen for an instant
Let life move in the distant

Revelry, as love, lessons learned,
and life passes discerned...

Change is certain as gravity
Creativity fills the cavity

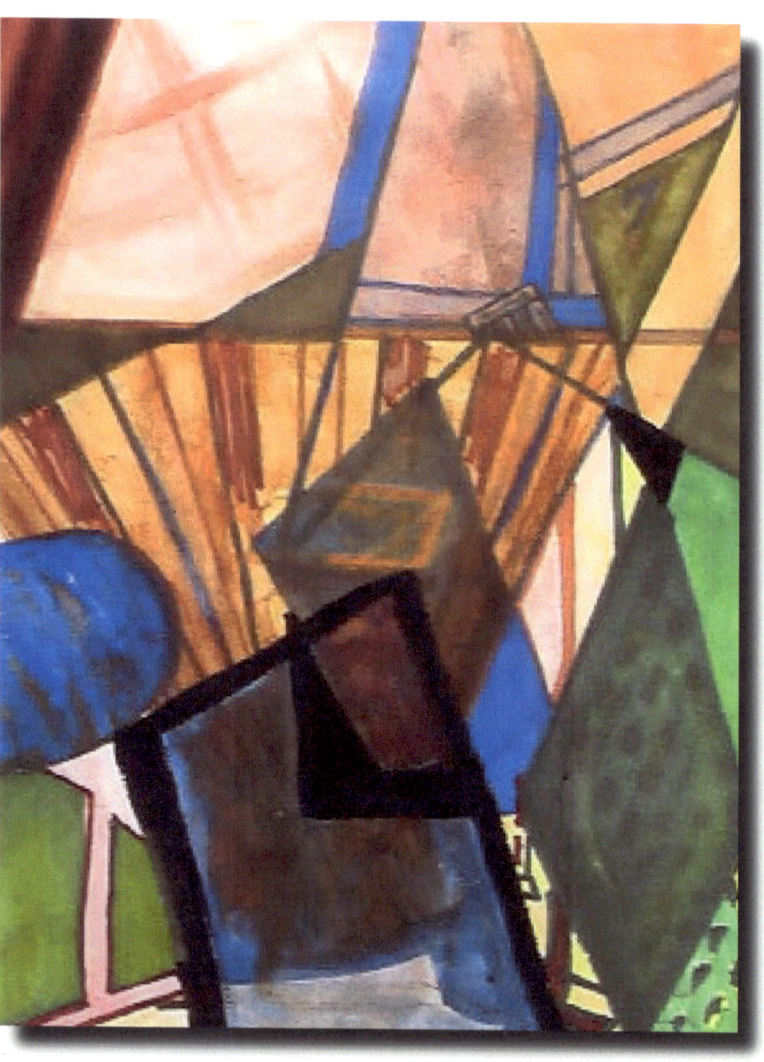

LIBERTAD

I am alone in Spain
a terrible feeling of disdain
I know there is a reason
not sure what it is anymore

I remember a time when I was free
A time when I was me
A time when I was innocent
A time when I was young
A time when I was beautiful
A time, a time to sing

So I leave my quiet place
I go out on the streets of insanity
I wonder, dodging through open spaces
Watching the crowd revel
The pomp and vanity

A time when I was free
A time when I was a zombie
A time when I was indecent
A time when I was ugly
A time when I was someone else
A time, a time to sing

A time when I became me
A time, a time to sing

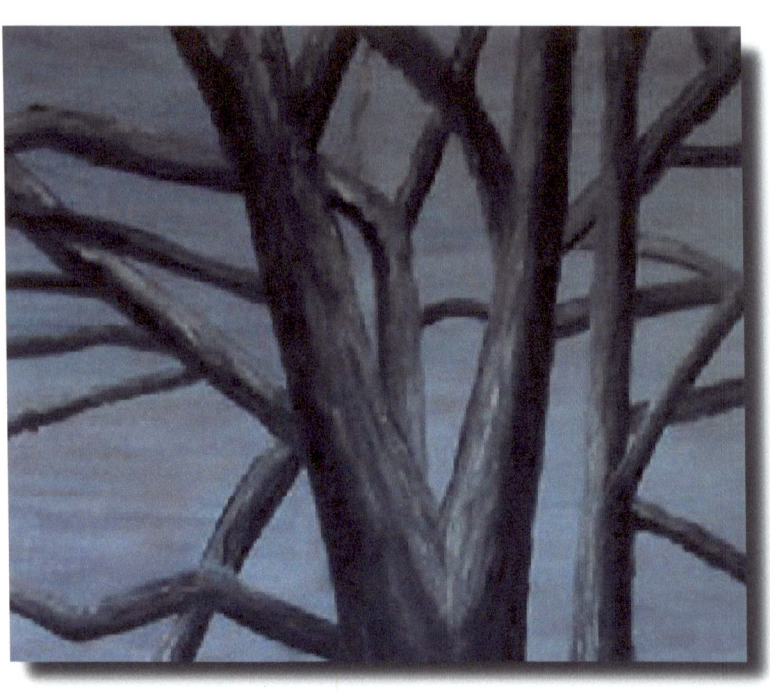

ENAISSANCER

Don't waste a day in purgatory
muddled in fear and uncertainty
Don't be afraid
Dare to fail
Don't procrastinate
the energy you put in
will come back to you
make only habits to keep
life will be what you reap
every thought that is true
comes back to you
options come streaming
like a tsunami of prosperity
you have the power - take it back
the road is not easy
it is worth it
Be discerning of false people
every thought that is false
creates shadows on your path
if one thing does not work,
try another
Don't give up!
I believe in you
The world will be yours
take the chance…

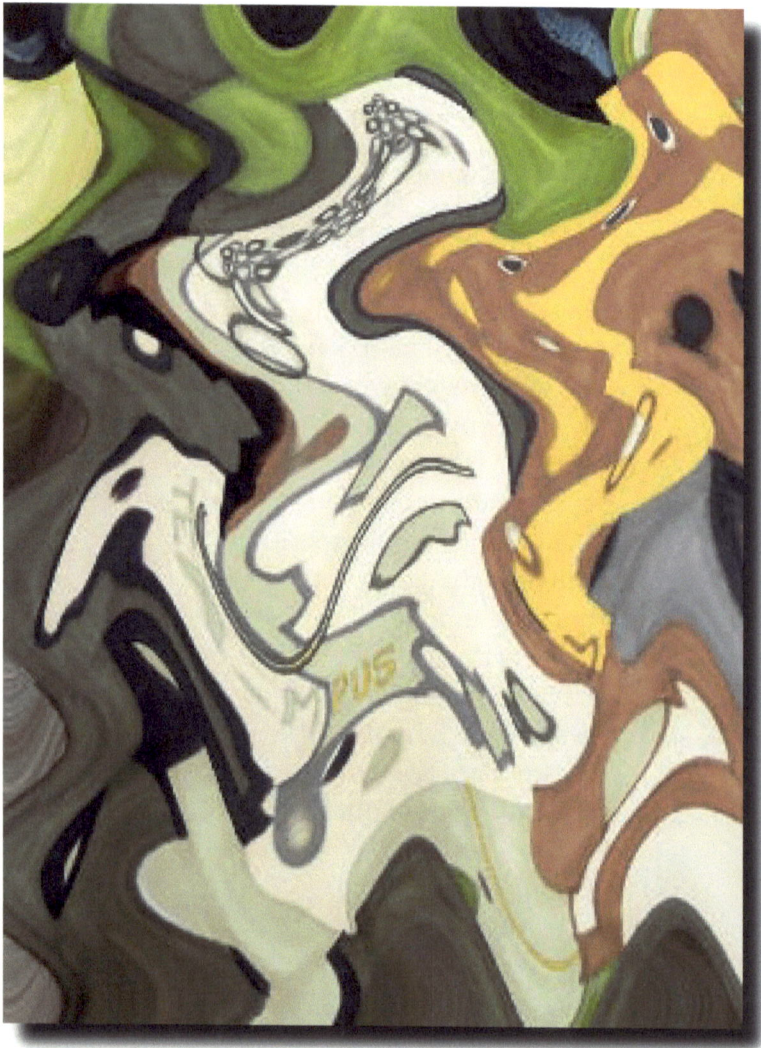

MATTER OF THE HEART

It is a matter of trust
It is a matter of what you want
      More and more....
It is a matter of the heart
And it is tearing me apart

Change is the hardest thing he says
Before he died that year

Worlds you never quite hear
 Then I felt that fear...

I question everything that happened until now
And I don't know what was real or a shroud

Forced to make a choice
to find my true voice

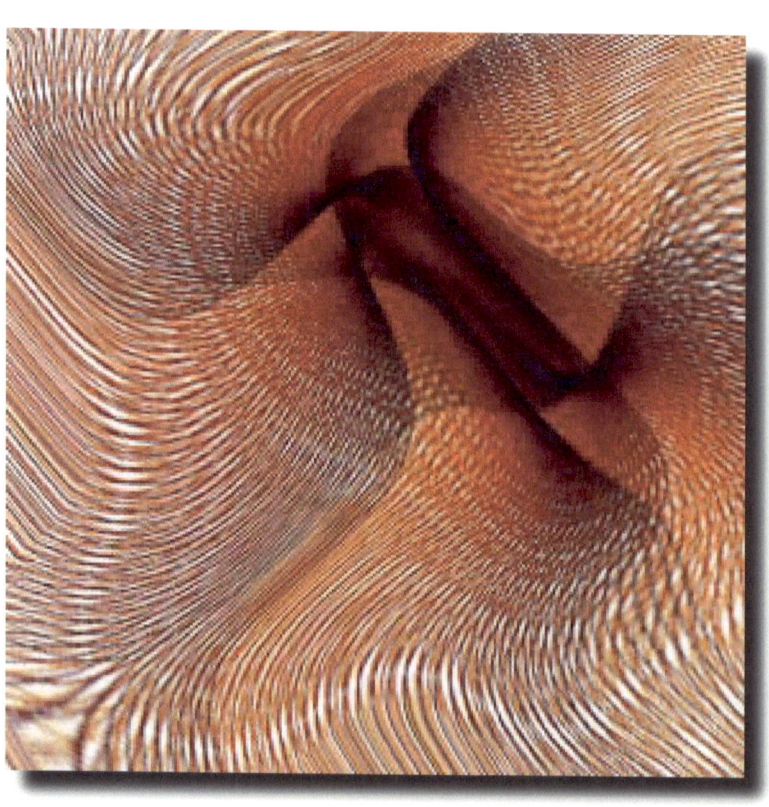

CREATION

I have worked hard going nowhere
Again and again and again...
I am so tired of waiting
I keep creating...
I just want to know
What will be, will be, will be...

I was so happy, I got the call.
All the pieces were coming together
The timing was perfect...
It fell apart day by day
Each day becoming more the same
They fade together into me
One day soon I want to begin...

I waited so long
The news was unexpected
I finally got a break...
I cried tears of joy
I danced in the mirror
Around and around and around...

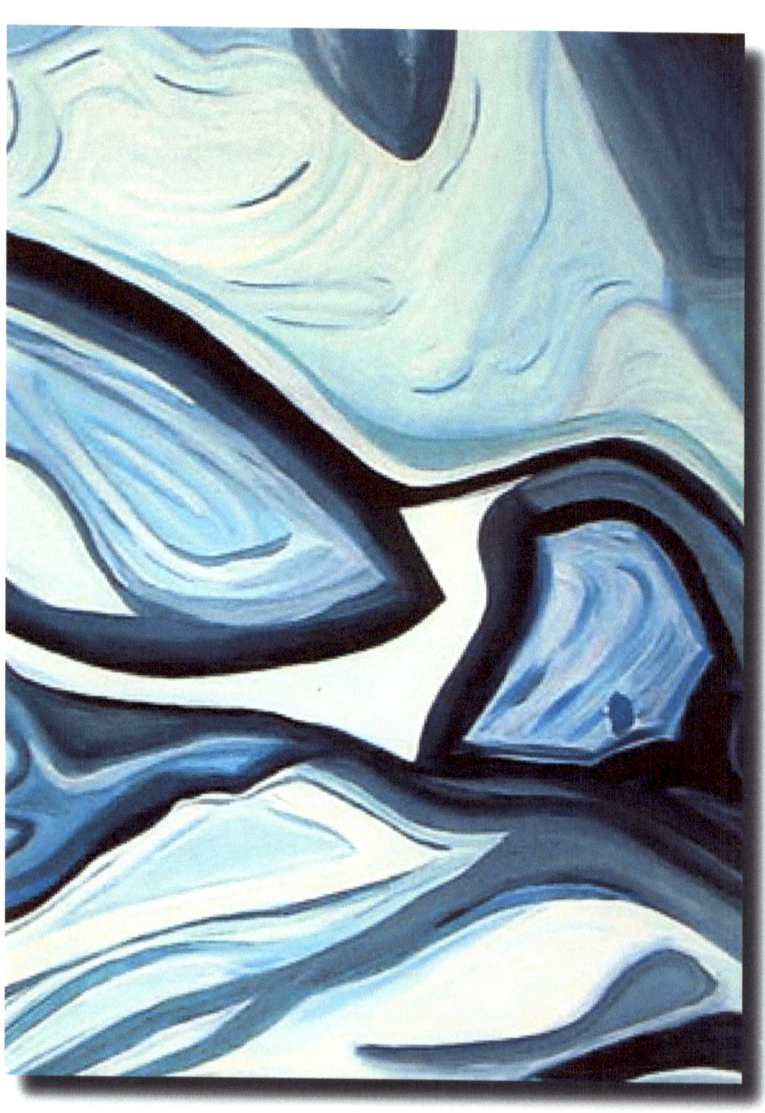

UNIVERSAL TRUST

Only artistic beauty
fullfills a certain duty

a literal truth and poetic realm
human reality and beyond

One made of flesh and stone
The other side is memory, energy, and spirit

The energy begins its journey at birth
freed and imprisoned over a lifetime

Consumed by lack of structure,
creation is more at this juncture
losing track of the days
an enigma in this haze

An awakening of the truth.

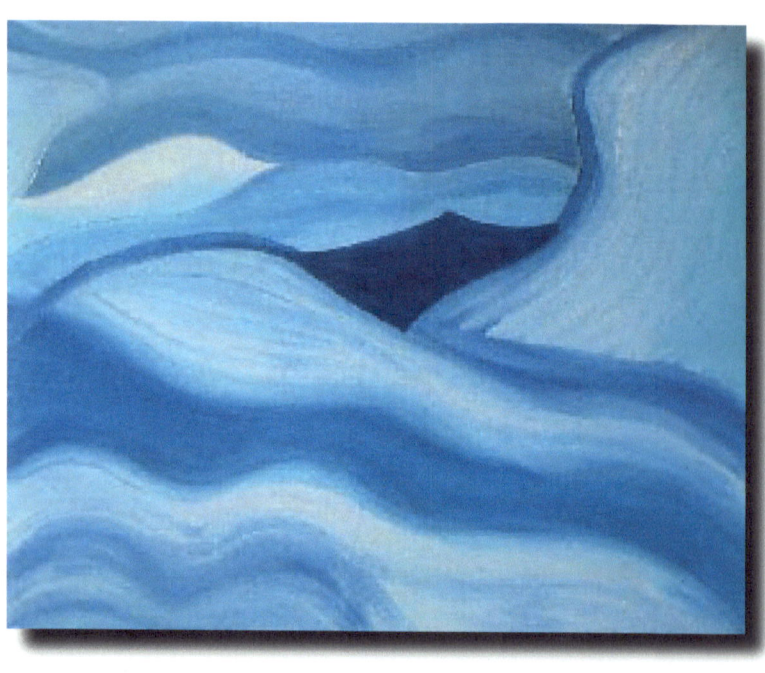

DORMANT

I was frozen for years
in a life consumed with other's fears
too afraid to act
too afraid of failure
like the chrysalis
of a butterfly
when I see them happiness
pours over me
it is the same journey
they make from
birth until death
yet their beauty is finite
reminding me of the full potential
that one hopes to achieve
it was such a dark place
I crawled from near death
to make my journey
always uncertain
yet there is always a sign that
keeps me on my path
each of us has our own
I feel complete to to reap what I've sewn

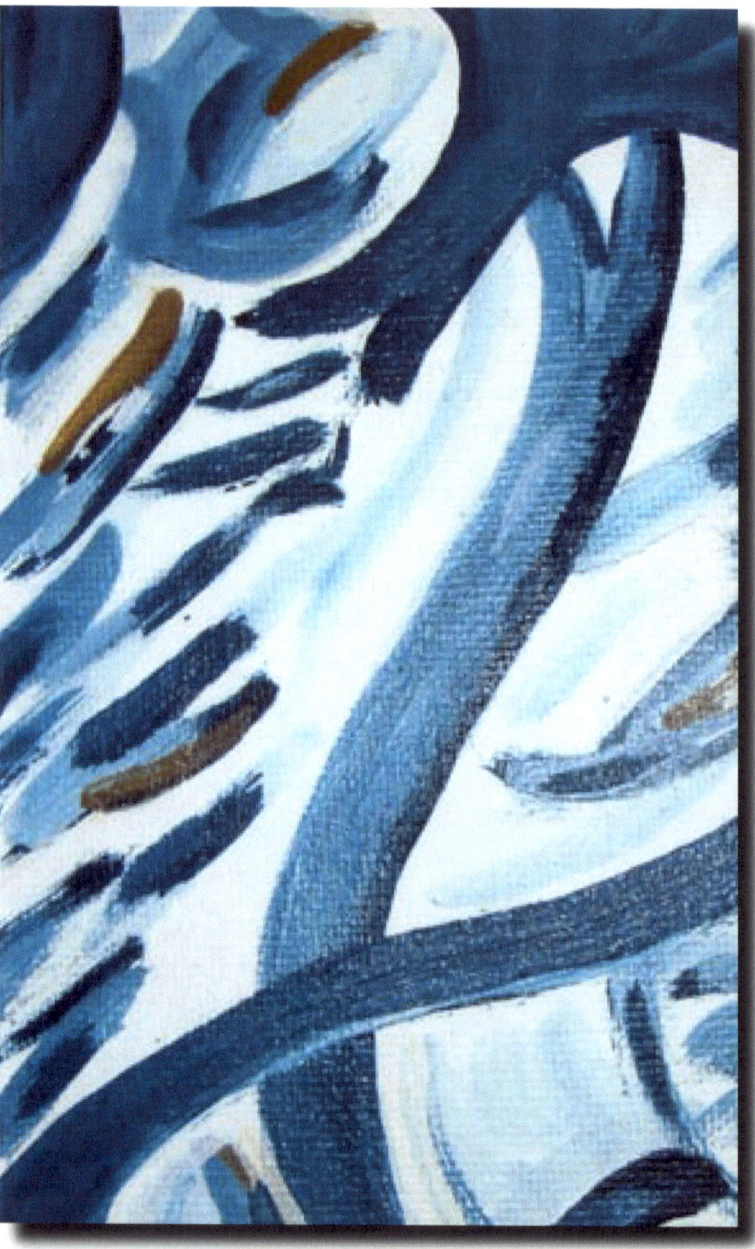

EVERYTHING IN BETWEEN

It is a rare moment of clarity
one can glimpse in rarity
through their own eyes the truth.

Our lives are clouded by happiness, anger,
doubt, absolution, regret
we lose sight of our next step

Everything in between.
time you lost in the moment

bonds you cannot choose to keep
remaining through time and distance

I don't remember the fights,
the reasons why or why not,
I remember the sound of laughter,

the only part that matters...

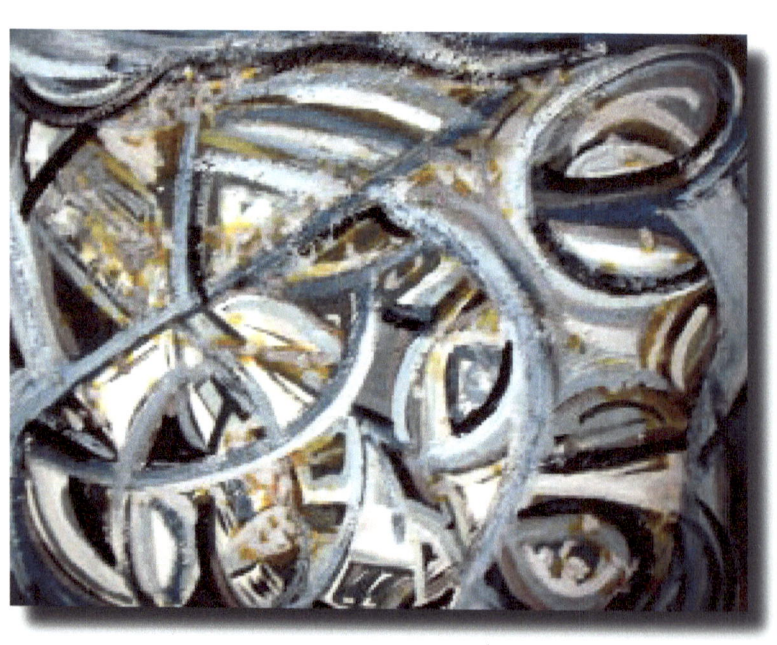

MY LOVE

There is not one finite love
there are many different types of love

Love shapes the people we are
the moments keep moving near and far

Love is unappreciated joy
Love is fleeting and coy

Love festers
It has magnetism
It lives in each thought
It is a universal inspiration
and cannot be bought

Love has repulsion
greater than expulsion
This love forever untold
Trapped in the confines and never sold

Love makes one vulnerable or attached
Love allows for everything and discards abashed

Love consumed by fear
One cannot stay afraid of something so dear

It is love.

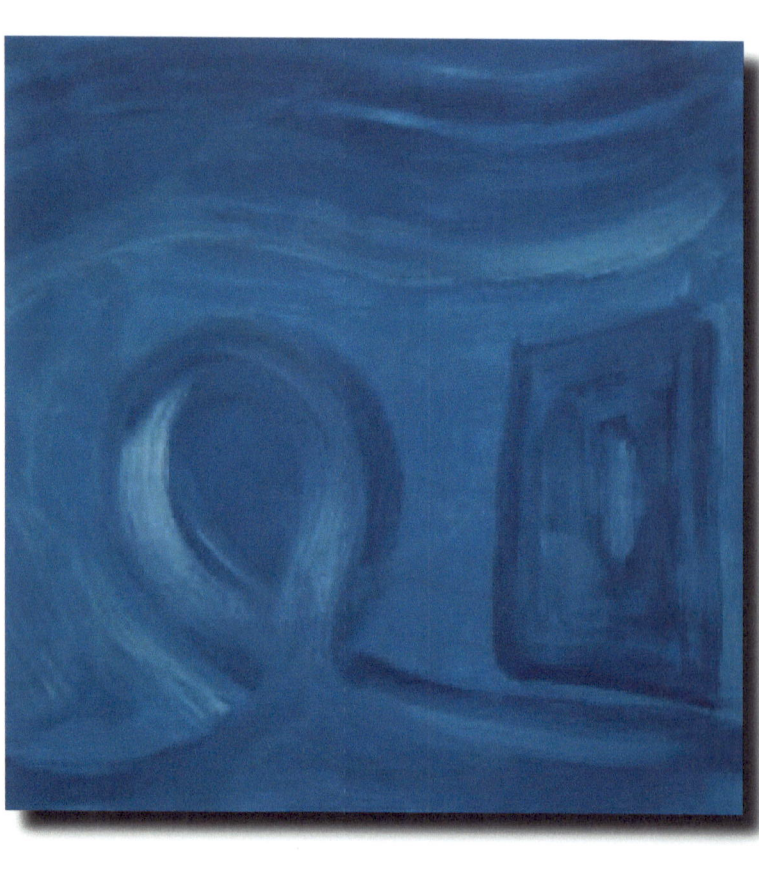

BLIND INJUSTICE

misapprehension of true freedom
guileless lives are seldom

Perpetrated disasters
enshrined in alabaster

proletariate will not claim influence
holding material superfluous

inconceivable to comprehend
the destruction from the sin

treacherous road of fire and ice
crafted by our own device

the injustice of indifference
sends a message to all of us

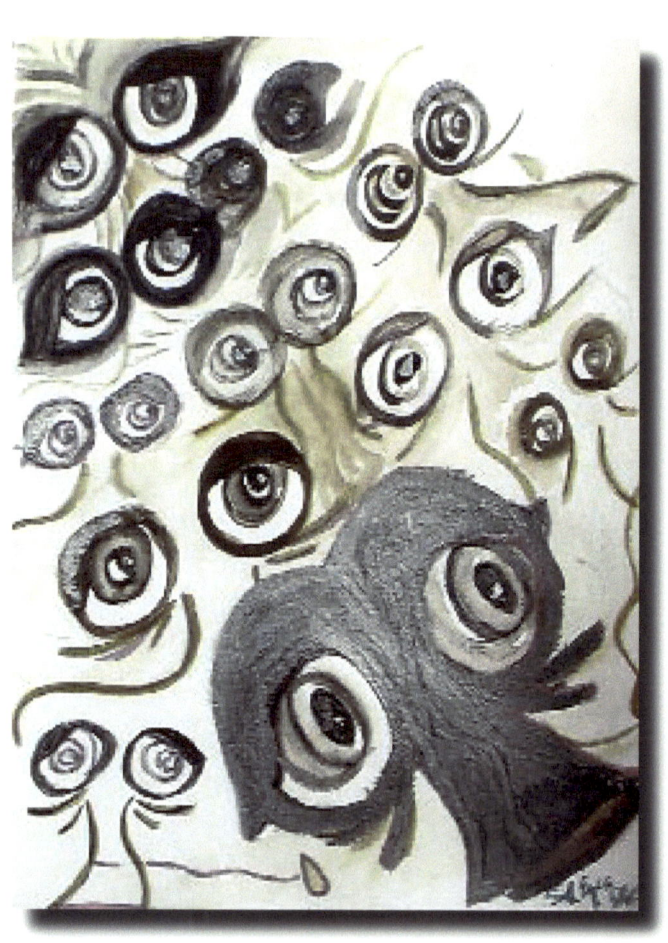

INSIDE TEARS

My head became light
My body heavy
The saddness persists
Just wipe the teary mist
The voice echoed so long
Just go on

It is easier said than done
When you think it is all over
It has just begun
Turn around, hold your head up high
No one will die
We must try

I have to be stronger
I have to do this for you
So I can breathe longer
And gain some peace

I went through the motions
Not even a notion
I nodded in silence
It hit me with no violence

You're really gone

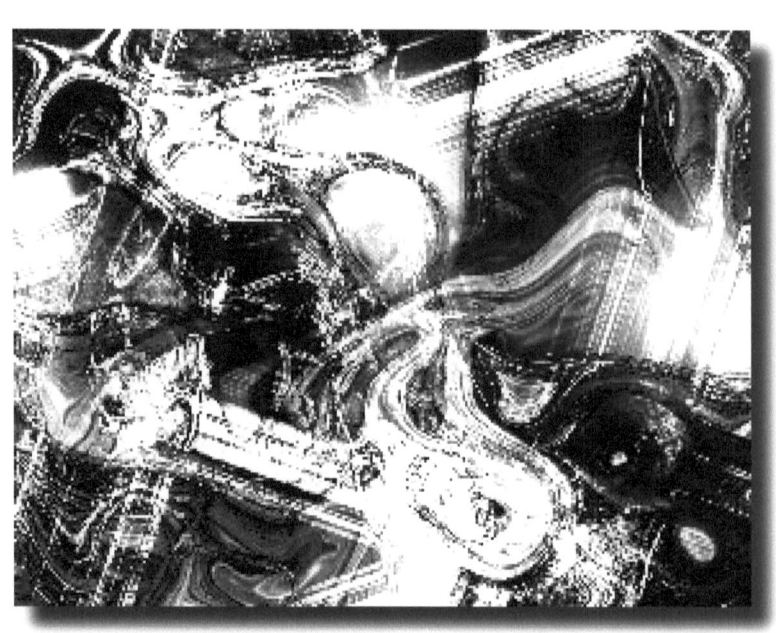

FORGIVENESS

I can't change the past
or lament to the last
forgiveness is the hardest to give
grievances hard to forgive

live and die through flippant actions
a shell of existence in caption
be fulfilled, is that so difficult?
defy the laws of man as a result

Live free, without apology,
Steer from negativity

Individuals can change the destiny of a nation
From I, we, and now us, no more relegation

Move forward with the strength of forgiveness
There is no need to change the path
A sovereignty in our shared empath

Wisdom + Compassion + Courage = Vitality

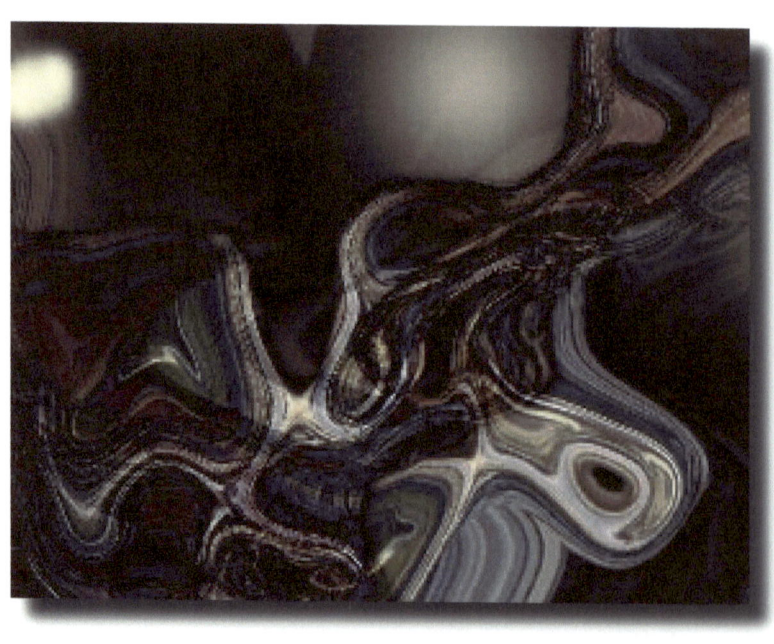

METAMORPHASIS

I never understood the reprocussions...
the darkness, the obliteration, or the rest.
Seeing only the good and the gold.

A part of me wishes to stay there forever.

Growth frozen in ignorance.

Ignore the creulty of the world
feelings surreal and unnatural

the end and the beginning.
I watched inside detached
It defied all rational knowledge.

Change started one day
it never ceased
Ever surprising revelations
All at once like a crash
until there was no trace

Different, yet better.
Everyday is an adventure.

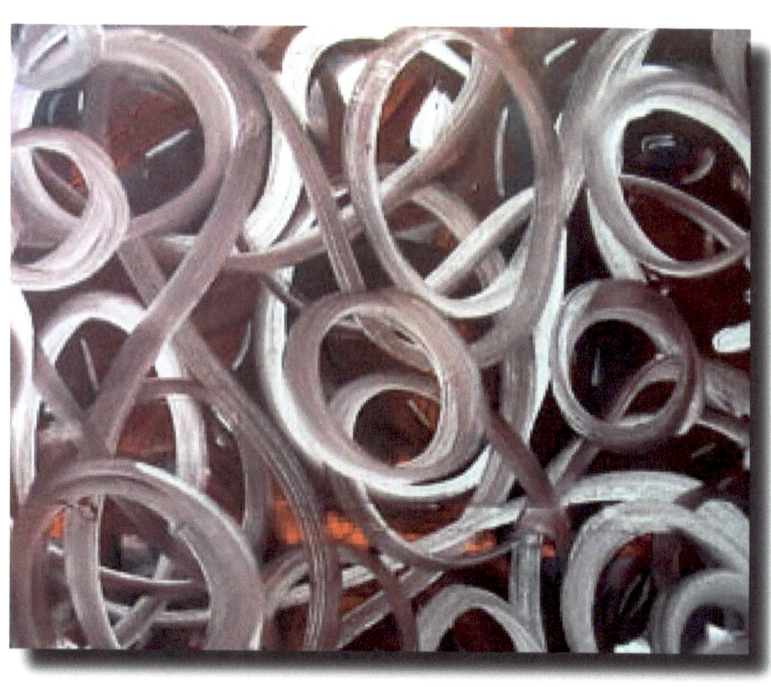

BELIEF

each person has to decide...
die and live free
live and die eventually

Proof would convince me for certain
delve into the world behind the curtain

my head in the sand like an ostrich
ripe for a predator to pluck
twisted soul, not wanting to believe
until no one could challenge that view

mindless correction of every word
resolute to keep writing
toy with my fragile madness

something that I could not refute
no one knows to be true or a proof

ubiquitous and silent
waiting for the possibility

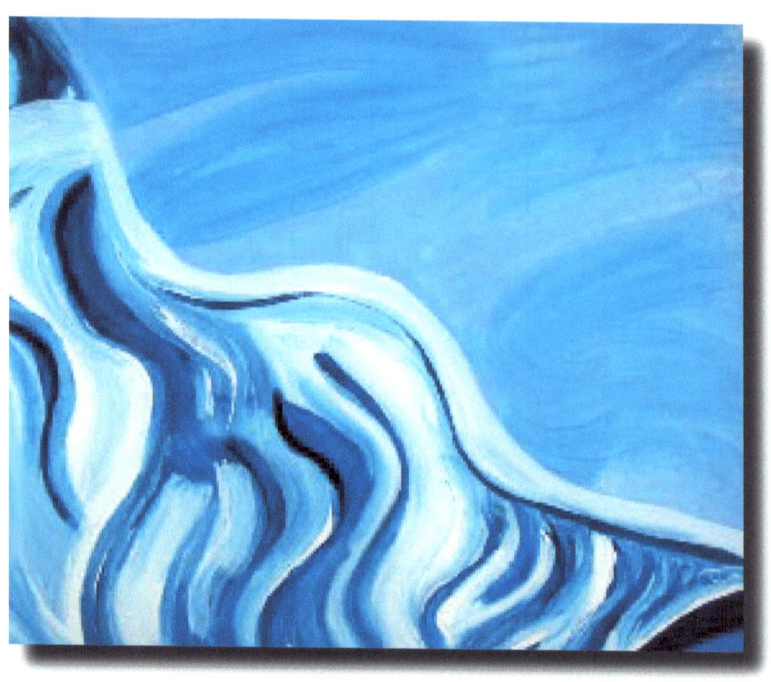

Realize that there is no time like the present to make a fresh start…

Everyday is the first day of the rest of your life, live each moment wisely.

Ava Leigh Stewart

www.ingramcontent.com/pod-product-compliance
Lightning Source LLC
Chambersburg PA
CBHW041106180526
45172CB00001B/135

* 9 7 8 1 4 4 1 4 5 6 8 5 4 *